Especially for

_____

With love from

_____

To Ellison, Kate, and Emery:
may you always abound in the creativity of the Father
—Jordan

For Uncle Larry and Aunt Pat
—Jonathan

THE CREATOR IN YOU

All Scripture quotations are taken from the Holy Bible, New International Version®, NIV®. Copyright © 1973, 1978, 1984, 2011 by Biblica Inc.™ Used by permission of Zondervan. All rights reserved worldwide. (www.zondervan.com). The "NIV" and "New International Version" are trademarks registered in the United States Patent and Trademark Office by Biblica Inc.™

Copyright © 2022 by Jordan Raynor

All rights reserved.

Published in the United States by WaterBrook, an imprint of Random House, a division of Penguin Random House LLC.

WATERBROOK and its deer colophon are registered trademarks of Penguin Random House LLC.

ISBN 978-0-593-19313-6

Ebook ISBN 978-0-593-19314-3

The Library of Congress catalog record is available at https://lccn.loc.gov/2020046176.

Printed in the U.S.A.

waterbrookmultnomah.com

10 9 8 7 6 5 4 3

First Edition

Cover and interior illustrations by Jonathan David

Book and cover design by Patrice Sheridan

SPECIAL SALES Most WaterBrook books are available at special quantity discounts when purchased in bulk by corporations, organizations, and special-interest groups. Custom imprinting or excerpting can also be done to fit special needs. For information, please email specialmarketscms@penguinrandomhouse.com.

# The Creator in You

Written by Jordan Raynor

Illustrated by Jonathan David

WATERBROOK

IN THE VERY BEGINNING, a long time ago,

God created the world so that we would all know

that He Himself is a *working* God,

though you might think that sounds just a little bit odd.

He didn't go to an office, a school, or a café,

but He worked nonetheless, much like we do today.

On a world dark and empty, He drew up His plans

to make oceans, the sky, and even the land.

With His work just beginning, He rolled up His sleeves
and built mountains and rivers and towers of trees.

He grabbed a big brush and painted the stars
and dressed up the sky with Saturn and Mars.

With just a few words,

He made creatures appear,

like polar bears, penguins,

alpacas, and deer.

God created the world in a matter of days,
a world for exploring, for work, and for play.

Before His day off, God had one more to-do:

on His sixth day of creating, God chose to make *you*.

And now you might think that our story is ending,

but in fact this is just the beginning.

God made you to *look* like Him—

to act and work and *create* with Him.

Because while in six days God created a lot,

there are so many things that He simply did not—

like bridges and baseballs, sandcastles and s'mores.

God asked *us* to create and fill the planet with more.

So grab a blank sheet of paper
and create with your hands
or draw up some plans
for a lemonade stand.

Roll up your sleeves and build epic tree forts,

and someday build cities and towers and ports.

With your very own brush, paint your own *Starry Night*,

or engineer a space shuttle and blast off into flight!

With just a few words, write a book or a song

that sparks inspiration or a great sing-along.

Create new businesses, movies, medicine, and hope.

Make laws or computers or a new telescope.

Because when you work or you make something new,

you are doing what God has made you to do.

You are showing the world what your Father is like—

a God who creates to bring people delight.

And when you show others the Creator in you,

you bring joy to the world—and to your Father too.

## Note to Parents

We talk a lot about how God is loving, holy, and omnipotent, but we rarely, if ever, talk about the fact that God is *creative*. Yet that is the *very first thing* God reveals about Himself in the Bible.

In the beginning, God *created*.

In the beginning, God was *productive*.

In the beginning, God *worked*.

All throughout the first pages of Scripture, we see God engaged in "the work of creating" (Genesis 2:3). This truth has dramatic ramifications for how we view God and how we view ourselves as His image bearers. You and I were not created to merely consume. As I say in this book, "God made you to *look* like Him—to act and work and *create* with Him." You see this clearly in Genesis 1:28 when God commanded humankind to "fill the earth and subdue it." This is a call to much more than just procreation. This is a call to civilization—a call to cultural *creation*.

I wrote this book because I was tired of reading books to my own kids that treated "the sixth day" as the *end* of creation. Day six was just the beginning! On the sixth day, God passed the baton of creation to you and me, inviting us to fill the earth with good things that would reveal His character and serve people well.

My prayer is that once the children in your life (and maybe some adults!) grasp these truths, they will view their future and current work with renewed purpose, enthusiasm, and joy. And yes, by "current work" I mean everything from home art projects to school and even chores! We are called to help our children see that work isn't a meaningless means to an end. It is a means of reflecting the character of the Creator God to the world and loving others in the process.

For more resources to help you and the children in your life grasp and respond to these truths, visit www.jordanraynor.com/kids.

**Jordan Raynor** is the bestselling author of *Redeeming Your Time*, *Called to Create*, and *Master of One*. He is a successful tech entrepreneur, a two-time recipient of a Google Fellowship, and a highly sought-after speaker on the topic of faith and work. He and his wife live with their three young daughters in Tampa, Florida.

**Jonathan David** writes and illustrates stories for children. Growing up, he was never far from a pencil or paintbrush. He and his wife live with their two kids in North Carolina.